GCSE REV NOTES I STEPHEN KELMAN'S *PIGEON ENGLISH* - Study guide (All chapters, page-by-page analysis)

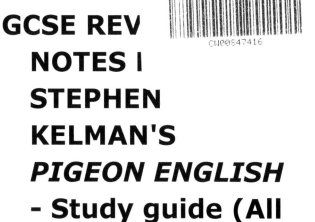

by Joe Broadfoot

Copyright © Joe Broadfoot, 2015

The right of Joe Broadfoot to be identified as the author of this work has been asserted in accordance with Section 77 of the Copyright, Designs and Patents Act 1988

ISBN-13: 978-1516805280

ISBN-10: 1516805283

Brief Introduction

This book is aimed at GCSE students of English Literature who are studying Stephen Kelman's *Pigeon English*. The focus is on what examiners are looking for, especially since the changes to the curriculum in 2015, and here you will find each chapter covered in detail. I hope this will help you and be a valuable tool in your studies and revision.

Criteria for high marks

Make sure you use appropriate critical language (see glossary of literary terms at the back). You need your argument to be fluent, well-structured and coherent. Stay focused!

Analyse and explore the use of form, structure and the language. Explore how these aspects affect the meaning.

Make connections between texts and look at different interpretations. Explore their strengths and weaknesses. Don't forget to use supporting references to strengthen your argument.

Analyse and explore the context.

Best essay practice

Use PEE for your paragraphs: point/evidence/explain.

Other tips

Make your studies active!

Don't just sit there reading! Never forget to annotate, annotate and annotate!

All page references refer to the 2012 paperback edition of *Pigeon English* published by Bloomsbury Publishing, London (ISBN: 978-1-4088-1568-7).

Pigeon English

AQA (New specification starting in 2015)

If you're studying for an AQA qualification in English Literature, there's a good chance your teachers will choose this text to study. There are good reasons for that: it's moralistic in that the text encourages us to think about right and wrong.

Pigeon English is one of the texts listed on Paper 2, which needs to be completed in 2 hours 15 minutes. Your writing on the essay will only be part of the exam, however, and for the rest of time you will need to write about poetry: two poems categorised as 'Unseen Poetry' and two poems from the AQA anthology.

AQA have given students a choice of 12 set texts for the Modern Texts section of the exam paper. There are 6 plays: JB Priestley's *An Inspector Calls*, Willy Russell's *Blood Brothers*, Alan Bennett's *The History Boys*, Dennis Kelly's *DNA*, Simon Stephens's script of *The Curious Incident of the Dog* in the *Night-Time*, and Shelagh Delaney's *A Taste of Honey*. Alternatively, students can chose to write on the following 6 novels: William Golding's *Lord of the Flies*, AQA's Anthology called

Telling Tales, George Orwell's *Animal Farm*, Kazuo Ishiguro's *Never Let Me Go*, Meera Syal's *Anita and Me*, and Stephen Kelman's *Pigeon English*. Answering one essay question on one of the above is worth a total of 34 marks, which includes 4 for vocabulary, spelling, punctuation and grammar. In other words, this section is worth 21.25% of your total grade at GCSE.

AQA have produced a poetry anthology entitled *Poems, Past and Present*, which includes 30 poems. Rather than study all 30, students are to study one of the two clusters of 15, which concentrate on common themes. There are two themes which students can choose from: Love and relationships, or power and conflict. Within the chosen thematic cluster, students must study all 15 poems and be prepared to write on any of them. Answering this section is worth 18.75% of your total GCSE grade.

The 'unseen poetry' section is more demanding, in that students will not know what to expect. However, as long as they are prepared to comment and compare different poems in terms of their content, theme, structure and language, students should be ready for whatever the exam can throw at them. This section is worth 20% of your total grade at GCSE.

Paper 2 itself makes up 60% of your total grade or, in other words, 96 raw marks. Just under half of those marks, 44 to be exact (27.5% of 60%), can be gained from analysing how the writer uses language, form and structure to create effects. To get a high grade, it is necessary for students to use appropriate literary terms, like metaphors, similes and so on.

AO1 accounts for 36 marks of the total of 96 (22.5% of the 60% for Paper 2, to be exact). To score highly on AO1, students need to provide an informed personal response, using quotations to support their point of view.

AO3 is all about context and, like Paper 1, only 7.5% of the total mark is awarded for this knowledge (12 marks). Similarly, AO4 (which is about spelling, punctuation and grammar) only accounts for 2.5% of the total (4 marks).

One of the difficulties with Paper 1 is the language. That can't be helped, bearing in mind that part A of the exam paper involves answering questions on Shakespeare, whereas part B is all about the 19th-century novel.

To further complicate things, the education system is in a state of flux: that means we have to be ready for constant change. Of course, everyone had got used to grades A,B and C meaning a pass. It was simple, it was straightforward and nearly everyone understood it. Please be prepared that from this day henceforward, the top grade will now be known as 9. A grade 4 will be a pass, and anything below that will be found and anything above it will be a pass. Hopefully, that's not too confusing for anyone!

Now onto the exam itself. As I said, Paper 1 consists of Shakespeare and the 19th-century novel. Like Paper 2, it is a written closed book exam (in other words you are not allowed to have the texts with you), which lasts one hour 45 minutes. You can score 64 marks, which amounts to 40% of your GCSE grade.

In section B, students will be expected to write in detail about an extract from the novel they have studied in class and then write about the novel as a whole. Just for the record, the choices of novel are the following: *The Strange Case of Dr Jekyll and Mr Hyde* by Robert Louis Stevenson, *A Christmas Carol* and *Great Expectations* by Charles Dickens, *Jane Eyre* by Charlotte Brontë, *Frankenstein* by Mary Shelley, *Pride and Prejudice* by Jane Austin, and *The Sign of Four* by Sir Arthur Conan Doyle.

Another important thing to consider is the fact that for section B of Paper 1, you will not be assessed on Assessment Objective 4 (AO4), which involves spelling, punctuation, grammar and vocabulary. This will be assessed on section A of Paper 1, which is about Shakespeare, and it will be worth 2.5% of your overall GCSE grade. In terms of raw marks, it is worth 4 out of 64. So for once, we need not concern ourselves with what is affectionately known as 'SPAG' too much on this part of Paper 1.

However, it is necessary to use the correct literary terminology wherever possible to make sure we maximise our marks on Assessment Objective2 (AO2). AO2 tests how well we can analyse language form and structure. Additionally, we are expected to state the effect the writer tried to create and how it impacts on the reader.

This brings me onto Assessment Objective 1 (AO1), which involves you writing a personal response to the text. It is important that you use quotations to backup your points of view. Like AO2, AO1 is worth 15% of your GCSE on Paper 1.

Assessment Objective 3 (AO3) is worth half of that, but nevertheless it is important to comment on context to make sure you get as much of the 7.5% up for grabs as you can.

So just to make myself clear, there are 30 marks available in section B for your answer on the 19th-century novel. Breaking it down even further, you will get 12 marks maximum the backing up your personal opinion with quotations, an additional 12 marks for analysing the writer's choice of words for effect (not forgetting to use appropriate terminology - more on that see the glossary at the back of this book), and six marks for discussing context.

As you can see, we've got a lot to get through so without further ado let's get on with the actual text itself and possible exam questions.

Previous exam questions

Notwithstanding the governmental changes to the grading system, it is still good practice to go over previous exam papers. To make sure that you meet AQA's learning objectives and get a high mark, make sure you go into the exam knowing something about the following:

- the plot
- the characters
- the theme

- selected quotations/details

- exam skills

Page-by-page analysis

Chapter One

Before the novel begins we are treated to a quotation from E.E. Cummings, which says: 'I'd rather learn from one bird how to sing that teach ten thousand stars not to dance'. It's debatable what this quotation means exactly, but it seems irrefutably to be about education. It appears that the writer, like Cummings, would rather learn a new positive skill than try to teach a group to ignore something that comes naturally to them. Of course, the pigeon is important in the title, so this suggests that much can be learned from a bird's perspective of the world.

An illustration of a plane follows, once again suggesting that the best place to view the action about to take place is from above.

The novel begins in media res (in the middle of the action) with short sentences to produce tension. The opening line: 'You could see the blood' is an example of direct address, forcing the reader through the use of the pronoun 'you' to be involved in the bloody scene (3). The narrative continues with: 'It was darker than you thought' (3). This presupposes that the reader has an opinion on the colour of blood. Its darkness in this scene suggests that something awful has just happened.

From the scripted dialogue that follows, we realise quickly that the action is set in the UK, as money is referred to as 'quid' (3). The use of slang suggests that the perspective is that of someone who prefers to use informal English.

Capital letters are used add to the impact of the crime: 'POLICE LINE DO NOT CROSS' (3). The narrator has a vivid, albeit inaccurate imagination, as we discover: 'If you cross the line you'll turn to dust' (3).

We discover that a policeman and the 'dead boy's mamma' are at the scene of the crime (3). The writer uses pathetic fallacy to show how the elements have sympathy with what has just happened: 'The rain wanted to come and wash the blood away' (3). However, the mother is 'guarding' the blood and won't let the rain do that (3).

We are told that a pigeon 'walked right in the blood'. Initially, the bird seems oblivious to the crime, but the narrator informs us that the pigeon is 'sad' (3). The pigeon's 'pink and dead' eyes are evidence of its sensitivity, according to the narrator (3).

We can guess that the narrator is of school age as we are told about a 'uniform', which is 'too scratchy' (4).

Some time has passed since the boy's demise, for we hear that the 'flowers were already bent' (4). The narrator has academic aspirations for it is noted that 'some of spelling was wrong' in the messages from his friends (4).

This seems to be a harsh world as Jordan wants to 't'ief' the dead boy's 'nearly new Nikes' (4). Alliteration emphasises how precious these football boots are.

The narrator seems to be more sensitive than Jordan. The narrator's religious belief is revealed by the following quotation in the first person: 'I said a prayer for him' (4). However, the narrator's knowledge of prayers seems limited as the prayer 'just said sorry' (4).

We then hear that the narrator believes 'a chief [...] brought his son back' to life by simply looking at him (4). Clearly, the narrator is incredibly superstitious.

The narrator uses a different way of spelling 'I swear'. By spelling it 'asweh' we get the impression that English may not be the narrator's first language (4).

We also learn that the narrator is a fast runner, if we can believe what we are told. The narrator seems fearful judging by this quotation: 'I just wanted to get away before the dying caught us' (5).

The narrator continues to use slang to describe the ninth floor flat which is 'not even hutious', or in other words, it is not scary.

We hear that the block of flats smells 'pissy' and that it's 'proper windy at the bottom like a whirlpool' (5). The simile makes the setting sound particularly dangerous. It seems as if the people that live there cannot help but be sucked down into a life of depression and or crime.

However, the narrator seems romantic about the wind, judging by the quotation: 'you can pretend like you're a bird' when the wind tries 'to pick you up, it's nearly like flying' (5).

It appears that the narrator is trying to educate us, as we are told that there are 'a million words for a bulla' (6). Through that, we discover that the narrator is a male, as he reveals he is in possession of one.

We also discover that Connor Green is a 'confusionist' (6). This seems to indicate that Connor enjoys word play and teasing others.

The narrator seems extremely gullible as he believes if you stay out on the balcony 'for more than one minute 'you'll turn into an icicle' (6).

The chapter ends with the narrator questioning what sort of person would 'chook a boy just to get his Chicken Joe's' (7). From the context, we can work out that 'chook' means stab.

Chapter Two

The chapter begins with the narrator saying that his 'Papa's voice' sounds like 'he's trapped in a submarine' (8). Clearly, the father is absent as the narrator says: 'I'm the man of the house until Papa escapes' (8). The narrator feels ready to take on the extra responsibility.

The narrator tells his father about his 'special' pigeon which 'flew in the window' (8). The bird can be tenuously connected to the dead boy when the narrator says the pigeon's 'feet felt scratchy on my hand like a chicken's' (8).

We discover that the narrator is from Africa and suffers from some racial discrimination as he reveals: 'Germs from Africa are the most deadliest, that's why Vilis ran away' (9). The narrator's poor grammar emphasises that English is not his first language.

We are introduced to a new word: 'Adjei'. This means actually. The narrator reveals that 'germs are tricky' (9). He is on safer ground talking about football, as he describes Vilis as 'a dirty tackler', who 'never passes' (9).

The 'calling card' runs out, so we realise that the narrator's father is calling long-distance (10). We can guess that he lives in Ghana's capital Accra, as the narrator mentions 'happy memories' of his time 'in Kaneshie market' (10).

The narrator is quite competitive as he wants to be the 'winner', when playing an 'abuse' game with his sister, Lydia (11).

He has morbid thoughts, imagining that dying involves a 'fire' which 'actually burns', unlike the flames 'in the shape of wings' on his Mustang (which must be a toy) (11). The wings link birds to death, again.

Chapter Three

The narrator discusses Manik's father, describing him as 'quite hutious' (12). The scary appearance reminds the reader of the pigeon at the start of the novel, which also had 'red-eyes' (12). However, Manik's father is kind for he helps the narrator with his tie.

We then hear about the games that the narrator plays. One is called 'Suicide bomber' (13). This name shows a lack of sensitivity, given the carnage caused by acts of terrorism. It makes the narrator seem as if he is living in a callous world.

It is also a world where there is a lack of trust. The narrator's acquaintances Chevon Brown and Saleem Khan argue over a deal they have already agreed over swapping watches. Saleem wants 'to swap back' (13).

The narrator claims he does not 'need' a watch (14). This shows he is poor, but not covetous. He relies on bells and his 'belly' to tell him what time it is (14).

Food is very important to the narrator as he says: 'wasting food is a sin' (15). He mentions having to 'finish' his food when he 'first tasted mushy peas' (15). He recalls this experience as he tries to learn 'about chooking' from X-Fire, who smells of 'cigarettes and chocolate milk' (14, 15). This description makes X-Fire appear vulnerable despite his violent tendencies.

Despite mixing with X-Fire, the narrator appears to be extremely sensitive as he thinks 'jelly babies' are 'cruel' (15). He thinks if he buys them, it will remind his mother of 'a dead baby' she once saw (15).

Finally, we discover that the narrator is called 'Harrison' after his mother addresses him during a dispute about 'a pigeon net' (16, 15). Harrison wants the pigeon to come back and hopes to 'make him tame' but his mother won't hear of it (16).

Before the chapter closes, Harrison links himself with the dead boy once more, saying: 'The dead boy loved Chelsea as well' (17). He makes football seem to be a spiritual pastime as he says: 'I hope Heaven has proper goals with nets' (17). The word 'nets' links back to the pigeon net he has just discussed with his mother. We get the distinct impression that Harrison's heaven is inhabited by pigeons and footballers.

Chapter Four

We find out that Harrison regards X-Fire's pit bull, named Harvey, as 'hutious' (18). Harrison is an unreliable narrator, to some extent, judging by his exaggeration that there are 'a million dogs around here' (18). He even believes that Harvey can 'smell' his fear if he doesn't hold his 'breath' (18).

Another dog is called 'Asbo', which many readers will be aware is an abbreviation of 'Anti-Social Behaviour Order' (18). It seems that Harrison does not realise that the name is an acronym. Ironically, this dog seems friendlier than Harvey, who has a more normal name.

We next hear about 'Terry Takeaway', who is a 'thiefman' and Harrison's habit of 'easing himself' on clouds of bleach in the toilet (19). This suggests that Harrison wishes he were in heaven, looking down on what happens on earth.

It's clear that Harrison misses Grandpa Solomon, a Biblical name that suggests wisdom. His grandfather claims that 'scissors actually beats rock', which again emphasises that violence rules supreme here (20).

Harrison returns to the subject of the dead boy, explaining how a 'lady cop' is asking about him (21). The narrator exaggerates by telling Lydia that the dead boy's blood 'was like a river' (21). Strangely, he admits to himself that he 'even wanted to jump in it like a fish' (21). It appears that Harrison believes that he might be able to bring the dead boy back to life by doing this. This provides us with more evidence that Harrison is superstitious.

The narrator feels the boy's death smacks of injustice as it was unlikely that he was 'ready' to die. Harrison says: 'It's not fair' (22).

Chapter Five

The chapter begins with Harrison teaching Poppy Morgan how to 'move your foot so the bass drum keeps the same pattern' (23). He explains that 'paradiddle just means drum roll' (23). Harrison enjoys trying to teach others although his knowledge is limited.

The narrator describes Poppy's hair as 'yellow like the sun' (24). The simple simile suggests that Harrison sees her as someone positive in his life.

The dead boy plot thickens as Harrison describes what the suspicious male wearing a hoodie who he can see from his balcony on 'floor 9' (24). Harrison sees the hooded suspect remove 'something shiny' from under 'the bottle bank' (25). 'It had to be a knife', according to the narrator. The suspect puts the object down his trousers and runs off 'like a girl with his elbows all sticking out' (25).

Chapter Six

By using italics at the start of this chapter, we understand the novel has a different narrator. We might already assume it is the pigeon that disappointed Harrison by not returning. The italicised narrator says: 'I watched the sun come up and saw the boy off to school' which immediately indicates it is not Harrison speaking (26).

The new narrator claims that to be 'perched on a windowsill quietly straining the remnants of my last millet meal' (26). The words of the bird resonate as it claims to know: 'the shape of a mother's grief' (26). It also claims that grief 'clings like those resilient blackberries that prosper by the side of a motorway (26). It calls itself a 'messenger', so we might assume it has a direct link with God, given its insight into people and their 'short' lives (26). This perspective suggests it's more than an ordinary pigeon.

Harrison returns to narrating duties, telling us that when 'somebody shuts their door too hard' his flat shakes (26). He pretends it's like 'an earthquake' (26). The image suggests that the consequences for actions are felt all around, particularly where he lives.

The narrator can escape his noisy surroundings to some extent, by simply turning 'the sound up on the TV to hide it (27). However, he cannot escape his home life, which he shares with his annoying sister, Lydia, who 'always acts like the boss when her friends come around' (27).

We discover that Lydia's two friends, Miquita and Chanelle, 'are both dey touch': Ghanaian slang for 'crazy' (28). Harrison admits Miquita accidentally 'sat' on his hand once, which has resulted in a lot of teasing ever since.

Miquita appears to be particularly unsympathetic when she says it was the dead boy's 'own fault he got killed' (28). She is extremely opinionated, seeing as 'she didn't know him' (28).

Harrison argues with her calling her 'fish lips' in reply to her calling him 'a little yappy dog' (29). He leaves the flat and goes to the shopping centre, where his mind drifts onto the subject of 'fuglies': 'a girl who always wants a baby from you' (29).

We then hear about Dean's theory that the CSI could solve the case of the dead boy. Dean explains to Harrison that the CSI are 'top detectives in America' (30). From this, we can gauge that Harrison's friends try to learn from what they watch on TV. However, they may confuse fact with fiction and vice versa.

The discussion is interrupted by Terry Takeaway 'running like a maniac' (31). Then we hear a butcher calling after Terry, who has stolen a tray of chickens. Harrison says he misses the chickens' 'faces' and 'eyes' (31). This is more evidence of the narrator's sensitivity.

Harrison is also intelligent enough to use words like 'ectopic' (32). He realises that the term refers to a baby that grows outside of the womb. He's upset about the ectopic baby's death and believes that if you don't have a name when you die, 'you'd just float in space forever' (32).

The narrator returns to the subject of pigeons and his belief that 'in England bird shit is good luck' no matter where it lands (33). Vilis says Harrison 'smells of shit', which causes a dispute ending the chapter (33).

Chapter Seven

The narrator's morbid thoughts begin the chapter, as he states that his 'coffin would be an aeroplane' (34). This image links him to the pigeon, which also gets a bird's eye view of the world.

The writer's use of pathetic fallacy further darkens the mood, as we discover that there is 'rain' at the dead boy's funeral (34). We see how superficial the news coverage of the event is, with the reporter continually 'stopping to get her hair fixed' (34). This adds to the impression that few really care about the dead boy.

Although his mother thinks the idea is disrespectful, Harrison believes the boy's coffin should be in the shape of 'a football boot' (35). The narrator explains that where he used to live, 'some people have a special coffin' replicating what they used to do (35). He also wishes he could have seen the boy's 'eyes' to see 'what dreams they gave away' (35). It seems that Harrison believes that eyes are the windows to the soul, therefore placing an awful lot of importance to this part of the face.

He returns to the subject of superstition, wondering if you opened 'an umbrella in church' whether it 'would give you double bad luck' (36). Harrison thinks this would lead to instant death.

Harrison adds that 'children aren't supposed to die' (37). He's so worried by that thought that he spits out his bubble gum for he thinks, if he swallows it by mistake, he might die too.

Some time passes before the narrative picks up again at 'the steps outside the cafeteria' that belongs to 'the Dell Farm Crew' (38). We discover that X-Fire is 'the leader because he's the best at basketball and fighting' (38). Additionally, X-Fire has 'chooked the most people', so the reader may assume he is a prime suspect (38).

The harsh setting is emphasised by Harrison's story of the 'chair car lady' (39). 'Two smaller kids' hitch a ride on her vehicle against her wishes. Even the sensitive Harrison describes it as 'the funniest thing' he's ever seen (39).

It appears as if Harrison has become somewhat unsympathetic to others' suffering, particularly as it's not fatal. Sounding suspiciously like Miquita, he says: 'It's the lady's own fault' (40).

The rest of the chapter is dedicated to a discussion about the rain. Harrison admits he likes to run in it and he dedicates his 'rain run to the dead boy' (40). Perhaps all his sympathy lies with him and Harrison has little left to shower on old ladies in motorised wheel-chairs.

Chapter Eight
The breakdown of 'the lift' is the event that begins the chapter (41). The narrator uses 'rock, paper, scissors' to calm his sister down (41). They are showing their 'Auntie Sonia', who once 'made Will Smith's bed' around (41).

Harrison hopes that his aunt will bring back 'Fruit Loops' from America, next time she goes there (42). The name suggests the slang word 'loopy', which in turn indicates someone is mad (42).

Through personification, the writer shows how sensitive Harrison is; he even sympathises with tomatoes , as he says: 'You wanted them to escape' (43). Perhaps they link to the dead boy's death through the colour red.

The harsh reality of life is revealed once again, this time through the story of Fag Ash Lil. Jordan spits on all the buttons in the lift and Fag Ash Lil is disgusted when she has to use it, saying: 'Bloody hell!' (44). Harrison describes the incident as 'very funny', which shows again that he is almost as much a product of his environment, even though he wasn't born in the UK, as Jordan (44).

Harrison talks about 'Colour Theory', which he has learned at school (45). He explains that yellow represents 'sunshine and Poppy Morgan's hair', green is for 'grass' and his baby sister Agnes trying to catch a cricket, while 'red is the dead boy's blood' (45).

Three drawings follow, as the narrator sees the funny side of signs. Harrison notes that 'there are warnings everywhere' (46). Again, it emphasises what a hostile environment he lives in.

Harrison's favourite sign is warning people off eating the watercress in the river. He believes that 'the water is acid', which would cause 'all your skin to fall off' if you fell in (47). This is more evidence of his vivid, yet erroneous, imagination.

The chapter ends with further description of the bleak setting: 'There's even no fish in the river' (48). To make it worse, he claims that the ducks were killed 'with a screwdriver' (48). The 'smaller kids' were responsible for their deaths (48). If we are to believe this account, we might suspect that one of the 'smaller kids' killed the dead boy. In this way, part one is ended with a subtle allusion to the 'whodunnit' plot.

Chapter Nine

Part two begins with an illustration of a thumb print, which seems to indicate crime detection. Perhaps we will discover the identity of the killer in this section. Above it is the word 'April', showing us a month has passed since the boy's death and the start of the murder investigation.

We find out that Harrison is quite reckless judging by his misguided ambition to 'sleep inside' one of the washing machines in the launderette (51). At least, he is wise enough to put off his attempt until 'one day' (51). Perhaps the launderette is the place to wash away sins, particularly if that means a return to childhood innocence playing silly games with his sister.

After telling us all about the launderette, Harrison tells us about a 'quiet' Somalian called Altaf (52). The narrator seems to believe the stereotype about Somalis being 'pirates'. This shows that ignorance is triumphant at the cost of education in Harrison's world.

Nevertheless, Harrison is trying to make sense of the news around him. He makes dangerous assumption based on limited knowledge; for example, he thinks: 'Dogs only attack people who are cruel to them' (53). Therefore, he logically assumes that a little girl, who was savaged by a dog, 'must have pulled his tail' (53).

Similarly, he assumes killers are easy to track down because they conform to the following stereotypes: 'piggy eyes', a smoker, 'gold teeth', spiderweb tattoos on the neck, red eyes and always spitting (54). Clearly, Harrison needs to be more open-minded if he hopes to catch the criminal.

Chapter Ten

Nathan Boyd is the first subject taken on by Harrison at the start of this chapter. He remarks on Nathan's bravery, but he doesn't jump at the chance to prove it by licking a 'crack spoon' (55). Therefore, we can assume he's not quite as stupid as he was portrayed earlier, in regard to the watercress.

Nevertheless, Nathan almost does go through with the dare, licking the spoon. According to Kyle Barnes, it 'wasn't even a suck', so he risks his brave reputation by not completing the mission. Nevertheless, Harrison still retains his respect for 'the bravest in Year 7'.

Nathan's perceived bravery is juxtaposed with Harrrison's supposed cowardice. The narrator is unable to set off the fire alarm despite his best efforts. His reaction to the consequent teasing is to 'feel proper sick' (57). He claims he 'didn't have the blood' suggesting that he equates it with bravery. He suffers from insecurity as he says: 'Adjei, my hands are too soft for everything' (57). He is quite harsh on himself and he seems to be confusing bravery with stupidity.

Chapter Eleven

Unfairness is one of theme of the novel and here is partially explored through the character of Mr Frimpong. Harrison believes that there's a chance that Frimpong 'sings so loud that God can't hear anyone else' (58). The narrator says: 'It's not even fair'. Nevertheless, he doesn't like his sister being 'disrespectful' about Frimpong, so his thoughts about him seem ambiguous (58).

Pastor Taylor tells Harrison that 'insight' means 'wisdom', so the narrator prays that the police can receive enough of it to 'catch the killer (58, 59, 58). As Dean doesn't believe in praying, Harrison prays for both of them, as they begin their own investigation into the killing.

They are going to need more than prayers, as they don't have a clue what they're looking for. Dean asks what sort of person they are looking for, to which Harrison replies: 'I think he was black but I'm not sure' (59).

Once again, Harrison relies on stereotypes and prejudice to find possible killers. He notices a man who has 'an earring' and 'deadly' eyes (60). He notices the man has 'a quick temper', a characteristic of killers, according to the narrator.

Harrison begins to refer to the man as the 'suspect' as the narrative switches to a script-format to allow the dialogue to pick up pace, without details of the setting and so forth getting in the way (60).

The suspect believes it's probably 'kids' that killed the dead boy, but like Harrison he's just generalising: 'It's always kids, innit' (61). The fact that the suspect smokes makes Harrison even more suspicious for he notes that smoke 'was another trick to make us blind so we couldn't pick any clues up' (61).

Chapter Twelve

The narrative switches to italics, which indicates that the pigeon is speaking. The pigeon is accusing humanity of killing without due cause. This narrator condemns people for treading 'on an ant' and says they should be more charitable and responsible. Finally, the pigeon says humankind needs more 'than just another invention of a spiteful god' to find a better way to live (62).

Harrison takes over the narrative again, relating the story of Kyle Barnes stabbing 'his compass in Manik's leg' (62). Thanks to this revelation, we have another suspect to add to our growing list.

It appears that Kyle is violent compared to many of Harrison's classmates, as he chooses the lethal 'AK-47' as his best weapon (63). Although, it is all hypothetical and Kyle does not possess such a gun, his choice reveals something about his character: that he wants to do things with the minimum of fuss. Dean and Chevon choose slightly less lethal options: 'a knuckleduster' and 'a crossbow' (63).

Harrison goes on to cite a list of random and mostly meaningless rules. He seems to value education as he states: 'The library stairs are safe' (64).

The narrator must crave safety, especially after he sees Dizzy take 'Dean's quid' (65). Nevertheless, Harrison confesses his admiration for the act, saying: 'If I was the big fish all the little fish would be scared of me' (65). He seems to be becoming more and more absorbed in the macho culture he finds himself part of, complete with its inverted sense of values.

Harrison and Dean then discover a mattress and toy with the idea of charging 'the smaller kids 50p to jump on it' (66). That idea comes to nothing, as Asbo relieves 'himself all over the mattress' (66). It seems that in this world, there is always something or someone bigger or more brutal to end your dreams. This may link to the dead boy and the futility of his death.

By contrast, Harrison recalls the simple goodness of his life in Ghana, when he helped his father to build a roof for his shop. The narrator says that sheltering under it when the rain fell made him 'feel safe' (67).

His father informs him that: 'One man's trash is another man's treasure' to motivate Harrison to give a piece of bamboo 'to a bush man' (68). Although, Harrison says the advice is 'very funny' the reader gets the idea that he has been brought up well and is likely to be charitable (which is a quality the pigeon thinks that humans lack) (68).

Chapter Thirteen

Harrison admits he wishes his mother was there at night to protect him from Miquita, who continually flirts with him in an inappropriate way. Miquita and Lydia are preparing to go to the carnival as 'parrots' (69). Here, we see a bird appearing less appealing to Harrison. This may because these birds lack authenticity; in other words, they are fake.

The narrator informs them that there is no such thing as 'a pink parrot' (70). Miquita replies by showing 'her tongue' to him (70). Harrison describes it as 'like a big nasty worm' (70). From this simile, we get the idea that there is possibly something quite tempting about Miquita, as the worm-like tongue is reminiscent of the snake in the Biblical story of Adam and Eve. It seems as if the religious Harrison is determined to resist temptation.

Lydia, meanwhile, does something very strange in the launderette: squeezing his mother's bleach into a washing machine 'all over the things inside' (71). It seems she is trying to hide something, but she claims she is trying to remove 'paint' from 'leftover bits of the costume' (71). Harrison is convinced that the 'boy's clothes' were in the washing bag, which makes his sister a prime suspect presumably.

X-Fire turns up asking Lydia: 'Did anyone see you?' (72). It appears now that Lydia is X-Fire's accomplice trying to hide the evidence, if we can believe Harrison's account.

Chapter Fourteen

We learn that Harrison is intelligent enough to read between the lines. He works out that the best way to receive a pass in football is by saying: 'Man on' (73). This shows that he is perceptive enough to learn that commanding others to 'pass' won't usually work (73).

He shows his charitable streak by letting a 'wasp fly out' instead of killing it. The pigeon narrator would surely approve of this action, which separates Harrison from some of his classmates, including his crush, Poppy.

Harrison admits to being in love before with 'Abena' (74). The narrator fell out of love with her because she's 'very stupid' and 'her eyes are too small'. The latter reason makes Harrison seem superficial. Clearly, at his age, no one expects love to be serious, so the reader does not judge the narrator too harshly.

It seems that moving to the UK has affected his sister as much as Harrison if not more as he reveals that: 'Lydia's always roaring at me now' (76). It appears life in Ghana was less stressful, but Harrison blames the change on 'too many cars' (76).

Harrison has become more acquisitive since arriving in the UK, judging by his admiration of Julius's Mercedes-Benz. The narrator calls it 'dope-fine' (77). He wants to buy one too when he's 'older' (77). Harrison seems to have almost completely bought into the values of the society he has moved to.

Going back in time, the narrator shows his reliable and responsible attitude by checking everything in their flat on their arrival, much to his sister's chagrin. Harrison tests everything and makes his own verbal inventory of the flat's contents. This is unappreciated by his sister, who tells him to: 'Shut up!' (78).

The harshness of the environment is emphasised by the 'greeting' he finds on the floor (79). The swear words show that the welcome he will receive in the UK is unlikely to be warm.

Meanwhile, returning to the present, Harrison continues to voice his admiration for Julius and particularly his 'ring' (79). However, Harrison's mother says 'only bogahs wear them' (79). Bogah is a term for a flashy wheeler-dealer in Ghanaian English. Nevertheless, he thinks he would be regarded as 'the ironboy' (80).

Chapter Fifteen

The pigeon narrator takes over again as it subtly voices its opposition to all the aggression that goes on at ground level claiming to 'fly over through the bluster' (81). The noun bluster refers to loud aggressive talk that is no more than empty threats. In the case of the dead boy, clearly one threat was carried out.

Harrison returns as narrator, telling us how he watched a free fall down on a 'rainy and windy' night (81). The pathetic fallacy of the weather conditions adds to the gloomy atmosphere. His pigeon witnessed it with him. He feels 'sad' about the 'bird nest' which fell down with the tree (81). He assumes all the occupants are dead.

However, he still has hopes of finding one of the birds alive. He has visions of looking after them, which ignites an argument between him and his sister. Lydia tells him that he doesn't 'know how to look after them' (82). Ignorance is bliss for Harrison, who thinks 'you just feed them worms until they're strong enough to fly again' (82).

Harrison continues to judge people superficially: he thinks the policeman who visits his school about the dead boy is 'too fat' to be trusted (83). Not only that, the policeman's 'detective skills' leave a lot to be desired, as he doesn't seem to notice one of the students pretends he is coughing but actually says the word 'pig' (83).

Pretence is very important in Harrison's world, as he and Connor Green compete to draw the most authentic scar. This emphasises how violence is a normal part of their everyday lives. Connor pretends his scar is 'from fighting a terminator' (84). Meanwhile, Harrison reverts to his roots, pretending he got his 'from fighting asasabonsam', which he explains is 'a kind of vampire' (84).

Although surrounded by violence, Harrison initially resists the temptation to become violent himself. However, he turns violent for the first time, when he pushes over a 'smaller kid' (85). Harrison does not feel any regret for his says: 'He deserved it' (85). The truth is,

Harrison lost his temper as the 'smaller kid' had the temerity to suggest the birds that fell from the tree were eaten, by saying: 'A cat must've got 'em' (85).

Harrison's feelings seem to be overwhelming him, as he says the hole in the ground where the tree was made him 'proper sad' (86). He doesn't 'even know why', so that suggests he has lost touch with his own feelings (86). He may be feeling extremely confused, which would possibly explain why he pushed the smaller kid over.

Chapter Sixteen

The level of disrespect that exists in Harrison's environment is highlighted by someone stealing 'the beer bottles' that were left at the scene of the crime (87). Harrison suspects 'it was probably Terry Takeaway' (87).

Chicken Joe worries that Harrison and Dean are 'going to steal the new flowers the dead boy's mamma planted in the railings' (87). Swearing at them, Joe tells them to have some 'respect' (87). This misunderstanding ends up causing a dispute, as the pair claim they are 'helping' (87).

Harrison and Dean are keen to find clues about the dead boy's murder, but they get sidetracked at times. Dean goes off at a tangent, describing how 'there were poppies' by the river last year (88). Of course, symbolically the poppies relate to the boy's spilt blood.

The blood motif is explored once again through the image of the Ghanian vampire as Harrison reveals that the escalator on the Tube is 'like its asasabonsam's teeth trying to eat you' (89). Through this imagery, we are subtly reminded about the murder.

Harrison calls the train journey 'brutal' (90). It certainly seems like a dog-eat-dog environment, with 'everybody [...] bumping everybody' (90).

The narrator's sensitivity comes to the fore as he worries about his Auntie Sonia's 'tree inside a pot' (91). He likens it to 'a baby who dies when it's still a baby' as this 'special kind of tree never grows', according to Sonia (91).

Sonia's fingers are 'like a zombie's', says Harrison (92). We discover that she burned her fingers deliberately 'to get the fingerprints off' (93). We assume that is to avoid being identified by the immigration authorities as

Harrison thinks that 'if you have no fingerprints [...] they can't send you back' (93).

Julius returns to Sonia's house and Harrison had 'to go' (94). Before he leaves, he describes Julius's bat, which is christened 'the Persuader' (94). Sonia has to give it a bath, presumably to erase evidence of violence.

Harrison is not tempted by Julius's offer of a drink, presumably alcoholic. Julius tells him to 'stay good for as long as you can' (95). The narrator wants to take on that advice and is moderately considerate when he holds in his 'laugh', when he sees 'a lady with a moustache' (95).

Chapter Seventeen

Alliteration makes the start of the chapter sound almost poetic, as Harrison says he can't see 'a barber on a bike' (96). This is yet another difference between Ghana and the UK.

He wants to have 'cornrolls' like Marcus Johnson, also known as 'Crossfire' (96). Lydia says that the 'Year 11' student X-Fire 'thinks he's the ironboy' (96). Clearly, Harrison admires him enough to want to have the same hairstyle.

He equates cornrolls with bravery. Harrison says if he has that hairstyle he will 'have the blood to pass any mission' (97). To be accepted by X-Fire's gang is very important to him and he seems ready to abandon his own set of values if he must to become a member of it.

However, Harrison is retaining some of his original points of view, when it comes to smoking, at least. He is quite pragmatic, being prepared to lie if it means he won't be pressured to smoke. If someone offers him a cigarette, Harrison plans to say: 'No thanks, I'm trying to give up, doctor's orders' (98).

Like X-Fire, Jordan appears to be another character capable of leading Harrison astray. The narrator lists all of the 'bad things Jordan has done' (99). 'Chooked some people' is on that list, suggesting to the reader that he may be the murderer that the police are looking for (99).

Harrison later calls Jordan 'a confusionist', mainly because he changes the rules of the game they are playing. Harrison was promised 'a hundred' points for breaking a bottle, but has to settle for ten.

He is so annoyed with Jordan, that he is relieved when Lydia turns up. Nevertheless, he is still so determined on impressing Jordan that he gives her 'a dirty blow on the arm' (101). Harrison tells her it is 'an accident', so once again we see that the narrator is prepared to lie if it suits him (101).

Chapter Eighteen

The pigeon begins narrating this chapter using militaristic language like 'blockade' to describe how humans block birds from what comes naturally (102). Interestingly, it refers to 'the rules of the game', which links it to Harrison, who has been portrayed as a playful character so far (102).

Harrison takes over the narrative, telling us how people used to believe in various gods; he mentions 'a sky god', which links back to his special pigeon (103). He informs us that 'feeding' gods was considered the best way of avoiding destruction. Clearly, humanity is risking the wrath of the pigeon god if the narrative so far is anything to go on. At least, Harrison is cut from a different cloth, as his generous spirit has led to him feeding the pigeon; perhaps he will be rewarded for his generosity.

Chapter Nineteen

Part 3 begins with a diagram of a CCTV camera; this suggests that the overriding theme of this section will be surveillance. The month is May, so now two months have passed since the murder of the boy.

The setting is 'the carnival' (107). However, there is a feeling of sadness as the narrator describes a woman who looks 'like a broken puppet' (107). The 'rain' adds to the idea that even a day of celebration resembles a day of mourning (107).

The harsh environment is further emphasised by the story of the girl 'falling over' (108). The smaller kids call her names 'because of the massive wet patch on her behind' (108). It seems as if the inhabitants of this area are brought up to wish failure on each other.

Even a romantic relationship is fraught with violence, as the narrator describes Killa burning Miquita 'with his lighter' (109). It seems as if any form of attention is welcomed, as 'crazy' Miquita laughs as if she's enjoying it (109).

Similarly, Harrison enjoys attention, albeit of a different kind. His younger sister, Agnes, seems to have decided that 'Harri is her favourite' name (110). Clearly, the narrator feels a lot of affection towards Agnes as he's particularly looking forward to telling her his 'best stories' (110).

Chapter Twenty

The bleak surroundings become even bleaker as Harrison reveals that his church is cancelled due to 'broken glass and bad words' (111). This relates to the theme of respect and the lack of it that exists in Harrison's environment.

There is more evidence that Harrison's pigeon is the god of this place, ruling the roost, as we discover the church is 'in the Jubilee Centre, the same place the bird was perched upon earlier in the narrative (111, 109).

Harrison's mother and Mr Frimpong wonder what the letters 'DFC' daubed on the wall stand for, but Harrison doesn't tell them that it's the Dell Farm Crew who are responsible for this graffiti (111).

The theme of deception is explored through the remains of 'Snickers' bars stuck on the window, which the Dell Farm Crew hope will look like faeces (112). Harrison concludes: 'They weren't fooling anybody' (112).

Harrison thinks it's a shame that the Dell Farm Crew can't go 'on fine missions' the way he and his friends did where 'he used to live (113). The narrator is realising that the set of values that he has brought up with are worth more than what the Dell Farm Crew believe in.

The chapter ends with Lydia running to their mother's room and crying, after Harrison confronts her about the blood-stained clothes in the laundry. She claims: 'It's a girl's blood' (114). However, Harrison thinks she's 'a big liar' (114). Some readers may be left unsure who is right, as her excuse sounds plausible. Yet, X-Fire did ask her: 'Did anyone see you?' at the laundry, so the suspicion remains that she is aiding and abetting the murderer (114, 72).

Chapter Twenty One

Harrison's attempts to be accepted by his peers has led to him drawing on his 'trainers' to make them 'look like Adidas' (115). However, he is laughed at, which makes his head go 'fuzzy' (115).

A more serous attempt to be accepted follows as he joins forces with X-Fire, Dizzy and Killa to 'crash' a 'target', to be decided by the gang's leader (116).

Unfortunately, X-Fire chooses Mr Frimpong as the target, presumably because he's 'only skinny' and seems unable to fight back (117). The target has 'to be somebody weaker', so you can 'knock them down easily' (117). Harrison feels 'sick' when he realises who X-Fire has chosen (117).

Even the weather cannot put a positive spin on what happens as Harrison explains: 'The sun came smashing into my eyes' (118). In a sense though, Harrison does see the light as he realises how senseless and cruel his actions have been. He sees Mr Frimpong's legs 'bent in a funny shape', looking 'like a bug dying in the sun' (118). This simile backs up the pigeon's view that humans kill other life forms just because they can.

Witnessing the subsequent robbery, Harrison can take no more; he speeds off. He describes his 'belly' feeling 'like knives', hinting that he may be in danger of being stabbed himself, like the dead boy (119).

The chapter ends with the pigeon acting like Harrison's conscience. Unfortunately, it admits it can 'only do so much' to help him (119). Nevertheless, it seems optimistic that Harrison will come through these problems intact, when it says: 'Home will always find you if you walk true and taller than those weeds' (119). It seems that it is all up to Harrison now to prove that he can stand up to the bullies.

Chapter Twenty Two

Morbid thoughts dominate, as the narrator returns to the theme of death. He discusses how some mothers 'kill their baby before it's even born' (120). Perhaps he is considering other things that he considers to be a sin, so he can rank what he has been a part of alongside it. He clearly feels guilty and is trying to deal with it.

Nevertheless, he seems to be of the opinion that the threat of violence can be fun. He reminisces about when his father allowed him 'to drive the pickup' truck (121). Harrison says his father wanted him to 'go back and hit' a grasscutter, whom he narrowly missed (121). It's only a joke, but Harrison enjoys the fact that 'it's only a secret' for him and his father (121).

Although steering a pickup underage is dangerous, in comparison to what he has just been part of, what he did with his father was intended to be innocent fun. Now it seems that Harrison is a victim of the unfriendly environment that he now lives in, as he says:

'the devil is stronger here because the buildings are too high' (122).

Chapter Twenty Three

The narrator starts the chapter by discussing superheroes. Unlike Ananse, from African folklore, Western superheroes 'never trick you, they only use their powers for good things', according to the narrator (123). It seems that Harrison is still looking for positive aspects in the environment he now lives in, even if it's in the fictional rather than real world.

Harrison needs a superhero to step in and help him, as he relates that X-Fire makes 'the gun sign' at him (124). Altaf's drawing of 'Snake Man' is not going to be helpful; it only reminds us that Harrison has succumbed to the temptation of trying too hard to fit in (124).

Salvation comes in an unlikely place, beginning when Harrison and Dean help Terry Takeaway extricate himself from Asbo's jaws. Asbo has the power to be Harrison's protected, as he tells us that the dog's 'teeth are like a shark' (125).

Grateful for their help, Terry allows Harrison to experiment on Asbo to see if he can 'smell evil' (126). When X-Fire, Dizzy and Kills come over, Asbo gets a chance to sniff 'them all like they were [...] meat' (127).

Harrison was hoping that Asbo's ears will go up to identify them as evil and they are 'still up' when X-Fire and his two friends head off (128). The narrator thinks the 'killing thoughts' are so tangible that 'they were sticking to us like crazy moths after thunder' (128).

Although, Harrison often confuses fact with fiction and is incredibly superstitious, the reader may feel that he is on to something. It seems as if instinct may conquer logic when it comes to finding the killer.

Chapter Twenty Four

The theme of religion begins the chapter, as Harrison explains that 'people who don't follow God are called non-believers' (129). He thinks a non-believer is 'empty inside like a robot' (129). Perhaps that makes them cold-blooded killing machines capable of murdering the boy at the start of the narrative.

After his mistake, Harrison seems more inclined to steer clear of evil and dark thoughts. Instead, he prays (albeit with swear words) and thinks his 'alligator tooth' gives him 'invisible power' (130). He thinks the special power is why his 'Papa gave it to' him (130).

However, Harrison still mixes with others who do not share his sense of values. Jordan proves he lacks Harrison's sense of compassion when he blasts a football at Fag Ash Lil, striking 'her proper hard right on the legs' (131).

Jordan's portrayal worsens when he shows Harrison his knife with its 'green handle the same as the knives from Mamma's block' (132). Not only that, he tells Harrison that he 'should get one' (132). To his credit, Harrison replies that he doesn't 'really need one' (132). At least this shows that Harrison is retaining a sense of his individuality, despite the peer pressure. Perhaps Harrison has learned from his previous mistake. He is not even tempted by Jordan's promise that they 'can be war brothers' if he gets a knife too (133).

Nevertheless, Harrison is still influenced by Jordan. In the privacy of his own home, Harrison experiment with 'the tomato knife from the block' (134). In the end, he decides it is 'too hutious' and puts it back (134). He decides it's better to be a runner than a fighter, as 'only Brett Shawcross can even catch' him (134).

Chapter Twenty Five

Harrison continues behaving like an improved character, by fending off Ross Kelly who is teasing Poppy. Harrison calls Ross 'skidmark' to shut him up, after he calls Poppy 'four eyes' (135).

Harrison asks Poppy to test his binoculars, and checks whether the view was 'close-up' (135). Poppy confirms it was, and Harrison seems pleased that the experiment has worked, as he says: 'I told you they were real' (135).

Although she's now his girlfriend, Harrison remains secretive by deciding not to tell her why he has the binoculars, 'if she asks' (136). He will tell her that they 'are just for birds and distant games' (136). Birds and games are recurring motifs throughout the novel, so this line alerts the reader to this.

Continuing to experiment, Harrison decides that he wants to know what it feels like to have 'numb' fingers like his Auntie Sonia (137). It could be argued that you have to feel numb to pain to survive in such a harsh and unfriendly environment.

After he feels how difficult it is to feel things with numb fingers, Harrison worries that his aunt may be 'burned up like human toast' if there's a fire at night (138). This reminds us what a sensitive soul he is.

By contrast, Miquita is portrayed as extremely insensitive. She seems firmly on the side of evil as she says 'the bad guy [...] don't have to ask for what he wants, he just takes it' (139). She seems to admire criminality.

It appears that Miquita's commitment to criminality may be more than just words, as she tells Lydia: 'You're either with us or against us' (140). The reader imagines this has something to do with the blood-stained clothes at the laundry.

Lydia's face gets slightly burned by the iron that Miquita is using to iron her hair. Harrison describes it as if 'all the birds fell out of the sky, dead' (141).

The image of birds falling from the sky is further explored by Lydia enlisting Harrison's help to tip her 'parrot costume' off the balcony (142). It seems like their dreams, ideals and all that is natural is spiralling down into the harsh, uncaring environment that that they live in.

Before the chapter closes, the siblings exchange secrets. Lydia tells Harrison she doesn't know whose clothes she took to the laundrette. She says: 'It was only a test' (142). In return, Harrison admits he threw his coat 'down the rubbish pipe' (143). It appears if both of them are intent on throwing away a lot of what they learned from their family and school in order to fit in better with their peers.

Chapter Twenty Six

The pigeon's words that begin the chapter sound ominous and threatening in tone, when he says: 'It's better if you don't see us coming' (144). It seems as the pigeon will be instrumental in the plot later on, although so far he has been mostly portrayed as little more than an interested observer.

Harrison takes over the narration again and this time the subject is his new trainers from 'the cancer shop' (144). He says: 'Poppy loves my Diadoras' (145). The underlying message is that fickle fashion has a hold of him and his peers, who are less likely to appreciate something deep and meaningful than they are to worship a trademark. It links to the theme of false gods.

His relationship with Poppy allows us to see Harrison in a tender light, as he informs us 'of the rules for girlfriends [...] around here' (146). In Ghana it appears you can 'chase them and make them fall over', according to Harrison (146). This is one of the few aspedts where the UK sounds the 'kinder' place to be, as he says in the UK 'you just hold their hand instead' (146).

However, his relationship with her is just an island of tenderness surrounded by a sea of destruction and malice. Harrison tells us of 'the lines' that 'you can't see' (147). These are border lines that mark gang territories.

It's no wonder that Harrison looks for sanctuary away from the danger. He believes 'the church is home for everybody' and you are protected by 'a sacred law' while there (148). This backs up the idea that he is as gullible as his sister claims he is.

Perhaps because of his innocence, he is quite fearless, when he has to escape Dizzy. He makes his potential assailant 'go red-eyes', by deliberately slowing down (149). He starts 'running for real when X-Fire' joins in though (149).

Harrison escapes thanks to the 'chair car lady', with whom he hitches a ride, much to the amusement of his pursuers (150). Dizzy and X-Fire 'were laughing like a maniac', which reminds the reader of the very real danger the pair pose.

Chapter Twenty Seven

Part four begins with a graphic of the sea, suggesting that water will play a big part in what is about to come. The month is June, so now it's three months since the murder of the boy.

The chapter begins with Harrison and Dean on a 'stake-out', watching passers-by for signs of suspicion (153).

Although the roller-skating 'Jesus' is not a suspect, Harrison notes he has a 'tattoo of a snake on his arm', suggesting the theme of temptation (154).

The pair of wannabe-detectives continue discussing what makes a criminal stand out. Just eating 'rank' burgers from 'the Chips n Tings van' is enough to put a suspect on their radar (155, 154).

Harrison has a list of 'signs of guilt' and to be a true suspect, the person must show 'three or more at the same time' (155, 156). This is more evidence that he is gullible, while craving rules to make sense of the world around him.

The bleak environment is emphasised by Dean's comment that: 'Some other kid'll get killed soon' (157). This reminds the reader how harsh this place; even children are pessimists here.

Finally, Harrison expresses regrets that 'the killer didn't see his colour [or know his DNA code] in time' (158). He naively believes that the killer might have been able to stop himself committing murder, if he knew in advance from his DNA that he had a propensity to kill.

Chapter Twenty Eight

The narrator starts by telling us of his sister's 'love': a 'Samsung Galaxy' mobile phone (159). Clearly, she has been affected by the materialist society she is now a part of. Like Harrison, who had to get branded trainers, she wants to be fashionable.

More importantly, Harrison tells us that his 'Auntie Sonia has a big bandage over her nose and her eye is all bruised a hell of different colours like a rainbow' (160). Perhaps because of his admiration of scars, Harrison finds something to admire in Sonia's injuries. Nevertheless, he wants to 'chook' whoever did it (160).

Julius seems the most likely suspect as Sonia becomes 'proper quiet' when Julius comes back from the toilet (161). She has to run after him 'like a dog', which suggests that he treats her no better than an animal (161).

To make matters worse, Julius lets 'the door swing back' as he leaves 'nearly' hitting 'Auntie Sonia in the face' (162). He seems to care little about her and is probably using her.

Chapter Twenty Nine

The narrator's tone is threatening at the beginning of the chapter as he expresses a desire to 'stick a compass' in Connor Green's leg (163). Harrison is furious with Connor, who claims he has seen 'Poppy's boobs' (163). Clearly, Harrison is prepared to fight against what he believes is wrong.

He then informs us of his commitment to Poppy, as the pair write their initials in 'Tippex' on 'her desk' (164). Symbolically, it seems as if Poppy is making Harrison see the error of some of his ways, almost like the way correcting fluid covers mistakes. It is also white, which suggests innocence.

Harrison moves on to the subject of sex and then sexual abuse. He thinks that 'the never-normal girl is always scared like a rabbit' because she is on the receiving end of the latter (165). Although this is just rumour, it still emphasises that children have to quickly grow up and deal with harsh reality.

The narrator feels 'sorry for the never-normal girl' (166). He wants to ask her to live with him to save her from her situation, but is worried about what people might say. It shows how affected by peer pressure he is: it can stop him doing what he thinks is right and encourage him to do what he thinks is wrong.

Meanwhile, he reveals how terrified he is of Fag Ash Lil. To avoid getting in the lift again with her, he decides he 'can only use the stairs' (167). He believes that 'the stairs are safe', which may indicate his ascent to heaven or heavenly thoughts.

While watching the TV news about the fatal stabbing of the dead boy, Harrison notices that Lydia is 'all sad like she knew him' (168). This shows her to be quite a sympathetic character.

The chapter ends with Harrison reasserting the values he has been brought up with: 'Manners cost nothing' (169). Harrison seems to have a good chance of rising above all the crime and delinquency around him.

Chapter Thirty

Harrison recalls when he talked to a pigeon, telling it he would keep it 'safe' (170). This leads to him discussing their value compared to human beings. He believes they are maybe worth 'more, because they can fly' (170).

His main concern is his sick baby sister, Agnes. He would like to trade places with her to ensure her survival, as he says: 'She can have my life' (171). He only wants to 'try Haribo Horror Mix' before he dies (171). Ironically, he seems to be surrounded by commonplace horrors everyday.

We are reminded of Asbo, when the subject changes to 'sharks' (172). He relates his dream of swimming in a 'black' sea, representing death. It seems as if Agnes is likely to die, judging by the negative imagery.

In his dream-like state, he discusses heaven with the special pigeon, who assures him that it exists. The pigeon tells him that Agnes will 'be fine' (173). It seems as if the pigeon may be able to help him find the killer as it says: 'I'll see what I can do' (173).

Chapter Thirty One

Ranking is very important to the narrator, as we've seen already. Now he begin to countdown the toughest Year 7s. Brandon Campbell is 'the toughest' (174). Chevon Brown is 'second' (174).

Clearly, Harrison has some admiration for the above pair, but none for Kyle Barnes, who is 'quite sneaky', and Gideon Hall, who 'has most backup' (175). Harrison has an innate sense of fair play and the latter pair are prepared to cheat to win, if necessary.

By contrast, Dean won't use his 'upper cut' because he claims it's 'too dangerous' (175). This makes him appear more honourable, whether or not it is true.

We then see Miquita fighting with Chanelle. The former fights 'like a man', while 'screaming like a crazy witch (176). Although, Miquita is an unsympathetic character, she has a lot of support from her 'cheering' peers.

Dizzy shows how callous he is, by 'taking a picture' of the fight 'on his phone' (177). Killa is slightly more sensitive at this juncture as he seems 'worried for Miquita' (177). Perhaps his worried that the secret the girls are fighting over will become public knowledge.

Lydia can't decide 'who to support' (178). Maybe like Killa, she is too mixed up in the whole affair to take any joy from the fight, which Harrison seems to enjoy.

After the fighting is broken up and Harrison heads to the Youth Club, Miquita is portrayed 'smoking a fat cigarette', sitting on the wall with Killa (179). Although he is not scared of the latter, Harrison's binoculars are 'smashed' by him (180). Consequently, he makes him 'suspect number one' (181).

Chapter Thirty Two

We realise how selfish people are when Nish and his wife get deported. Rather than worry about their welfare, 'all the women were very worried for if they couldn't get their meat anymore' (182).

We discover that Nish is Pakistani and that Harrison admires the national flag of that country because it has a star on it. To him that represents 'freedom' (183). It seems unjust that he is being deported purely because he and his wife are 'illegal' immigrants (183). They clearly played an important part in the community. Although Harrison worries about them, he seems more worried about his own status, asking Lydia if their 'visa works' or not (184).

He moves back onto his attempts to extract DNA from suspects. He saying 'lying is ok if it's for a good reason', trying to get Jordan to give him a saliva sample, ostensibly for a science experiment (185).

His attempt is unsuccessful and the conversation moves on to guns. Jordan's favourite is a 'Glock', whereas Harrison's is a 'supersoaker' (186). This juxtaposition shows how different they are. Harrison appears to have been brought up better and is less inclined to be violent.

Jordan 'had to bury a gun' for the Dell Farm Crew (187). This shows he is nothing more than their lackey.

Meanwhile, Harrison fantasises about burying a gun and selling all the 'baby guns' that grow out of the soil (188). This romantic notion makes him a more sympathetic character than Jordan.

However, Harrison is influenced by Jordan. So much so, he is spotted throwing stones at a bus by his mother, who starts 'pushing' him towards home (189).

The chapter ends with Jordan spitting in Harrison's 'face', with the narrator being 'sounded' by his mother, or soundly beaten in other words. Interestingly, the narrator does not explain Ghanian terms to the reader: perhaps this indicates the implied listener is a new arrival from Ghana, who only needs English terms explained.

Chapter Thirty Three

The pigeon's contemptuous tone begins the narrative as using direct address he says: 'Your superstitions tickle me' (191). We wonder if he will be a merciful god with this attitude.

Harrison takes over the narrative, telling us about 'an important mission' that he undertook with his father and Patrick Kuffour in Ghana (192). Unlike the UK, his missions there are to help people: 'filling up everybody's lanterns with paraffin' during a blackout.

Back in the UK, Harrison thanks the pigeon 'for showing' him the 'right star', when he was stargazing earlier in the chapter (193). He drops his 'alligator tooth down the rubbish pipe' as an 'offering for the volcano god' (193). He certainly wants divine intervention to lead him in the right direction, as since leaving Ghana, he has become involved with some unsavoury characters, like Jordan.

Chapter Thirty Four

Harrison's superstitious beliefs make him think that by standing 'on the church grass' he will be safe from his foes (194). Dizzy makes it clear that he doesn't believe in 'fairy stories', belittling Harrison's beliefs.

Nevertheless, Harrison has not given up on his chance of getting some finger prints. This shows he's an opportunist, as he's ready to seize the chance when Dizzy pushes Killa 'up against the window' (195).

Killa is described as 'like a rat lost in a tunnel', as his fingerprints are taken and he doesn't know who to chase after (196). The 'rat' description makes him sound like an animal that inhabits drains and dirty places, adding to the idea that he is dangerous.

Later, Dean shows Harrison 'a snake eating a boy' on YouTube (197). The motif of the snake keeps reappearing, reminding us how hostile the modern world can be. Although the serpent is part of the natural world, YouTube is, of course, part of the modern digital world that may desensitise people.

Harrison imagines Killa as a 'snake boy', who might turn into a dangerous 'Snake Man' (198). He enjoys his sense of power as now that he has the fingerprints it's like he owns a 'piece of Killa's life' (198).

Finally, he imagines Agnes growing up to be a superhero, saying: 'When she grows up she'll be called SuperShouter' (199). She's a positive influence on him, although she's just a baby. If she and his father weren't so far away, perhaps Harrison would be less prone to forget the values he was brought up with as he'd have a greater sense of family.

Chapter Thirty Five

The chapter opens by showing us a glimpse of Julius's business, as we see 'a big pile of passports on the table' (200). He's trading on other people's misfortune and his continual slapping of Aunt Sonia's 'behind' makes him appear even more unsavoury (200).

Ironically, Julius does have a 'gentle' side, as we see him 'fixing the Persuader', his weapon of choice (201). He treats the bat like it 'was a one-leg pigeon' (201). Perhaps we can say he worships it, in that case, as Harrison's special pigeon has god-like status in the novel.

Julius seems proud of the damage he's inflicted on people with the weapon, admitting that after he hit someone on the head 'it was like a light switching off' (202). Julius represents darkness and evil, especially as he does his 'big messy laugh' after saying that one of the victims is 'a vegetable now' (202).

Meanwhile, back at school, Harrison is confronted by Killa in the toilets. Killa threatens him with 'a craft knife', which is ironic as something artistic is being used destructively (203).

Unlike the 'vegetable' mentioned earlier, 'light' appears rather than disappears when the attack begins (203, 204). If we equate light with consciousness, this gives us hope that Harrison will come through virtually unscathed. Harrison only ends up with 'a black smudge' on his shirt 'from Killa's dirty hands' (204).

Harrison's inquiring mind is in evidence again soon afterwards, as he wants to 'test' his sister's birthday present. He puts her earrings in his mouth, as he says 'if there's no teeth marks left behind it's real gold' (205).

His other sister, Agnes, has been attempting to write her name. It comes out 'all lovely and wobbly like a spider wrote it' (206). Using natural imagery, Harrison conveys the idea that Agnes is as fascinating as a spider.

Meanwhile, Harrison pressures Lydia into doing what he wants her to, calling her a 'scaredy cat' when she is reluctant initially (207). He unwisely gets her to join him in putting her 'footprints' in some wet cement (208). This reminds us of the fingerprints he has taken from Killa, although this is more permanent. It's a strange birthday present, although Lydia screams 'like a baby' which suggests she's excited (209).

The chapter ends with the pigeon taking over the narrative. It makes it sound as if humans are insignificant in the greater scheme of things, as it says: 'You're not the sea, you're just a raindrop' (210).

Chapter Thirty Six

Harrison's continual quest to find superhero qualities in others starts the chapter on a positive note. He describes Manik as 'Superhands' because of his exploits in goal (211). Meanwhile, Dean is called 'Monkey Blood' because he's such a good climber (211).

We feel a significant moment is coming, as when Harrison looks up at Dean on the top of the garage he hears 'wings' (212). This seems to be a message from the pigeon.

Dean finds a picture of 'the dead ball' with his 'girlfriend' (212, 213). Harrison compares the girlfriend to Poppy, reminding us that the dead boy could have just as easily been him.

The dead boy could be forgotten by many now as 'the hole where the tree used to be is all the way gone' (214). Although the tree doesn't relate directly to the boy, it does show us how quickly life moves on. We can assume that the earth where the boy is buried is also 'covered now' with 'grass', 'plants and weeds' (214).

To end the chapter, Harrison enjoys his sense of power over Asbo, when Terry allows him to hold his lead. Harrison says it feels 'like I owned him' (215).

Chapter Thirty Seven

Part five begins with a graphic of a pigeon and July. It seems the bird may play a big part in identifying the killer, four months after the murder.

The chapter begins with the narrator reiterating the importance of fingerprints, which 'are just for feeling with and to help you hold onto things when they're wet' (219). Additionally, they are important for identifying criminals, which is why Harrison has tried so hard to get the fingerprints of suspects. It is almost as if he is downplaying their importance somewhat, at this juncture, as he uses the word 'just' (219). Perhaps his hopes of finding the killer are diminishing.

Harrison talks about his 'beach buggy' and how the 'floor outside' his flat 'is perfect for driving' (220). He uses his toy to tempt Jordan into becoming friends with him again. He admits he wants 'to punish' Jordan (221). He won't let Jordan play with it and says it feels 'brilliant' (221). Clearly, he enjoys a sense of power over Jordan.

He loses this sense of power when Miquita teaches him how to kiss. He says she looks 'like a frog', but also refers to her 'expert lips (222). This shows his feelings towards her are ambiguous: he's attracted yet nauseated by her.

She represents temptation, which is obvious when her tongue is depicted 'twisting around' in Harrison's mouth 'like a nasty snake' (223).

He thinks of Poppy's 'yellow', which fills him up 'like the sun' (223). Poppy is clearly a positive force on him, but her rays of sunshine cannot reach him in the dark thoughts of Miquita, which he finds himself engulfed in.

He describes his belly feeling 'sick like the sea' (224). His skin is 'crawling' afterwards 'with hair tickles' after this encounter. He seems traumatised.

Lydia's outburst when she says to Miquita: 'At least my boyfriend's not a murderer' changes their relationship (225). There is no way back for them. Harrison has some sympathy for Miquita, saying: 'You couldn't hate her fat burny hands anymore' (225). He adds that 'Miquita didn't know what to do, she just split proper quiet' (226). This is quite a dignified exit for a character who has been portrayed as close to evil so far.

Chapter Thirty Eight

The pigeon begins the narrative by telling us how he has inside knowledge of the dreams of 'the lady who drives the chair' (227). These dreams partially relate to the sea, with 'seahorses nibbling at her tender toes' (227).

We then realise that the pigeon is being assaulted by four other birds that come 'from nowhere' (227). Changing the narrative perspective, Harrison reports how he jumps in to scatter the magpies and rescue his special pigeon.

Materialism, albeit a harmless version, comes to the fore as Harrison tells us he gives 'Poppy a Jelly Ring' (228). He adds that it is his 'secret sorry for kissing Miquita' (228). He clearly feels guilty for what he has done.

Just as important as Poppy is his quest to be 'the best runner' (229). He has to imagine that the others will tear him 'into little pieces' if they catch him, in order to get the most out of himself (230).

What really gets him across the line in front of Brett Shawcross is 'the spirit' in his trainers (231). We feel some sympathy for him as he 'only' has Diadoras, whereas 'Brett Shawcross has Nikes' (230). The disadvantaged underdog wins the race, which gives the reader some satisfaction, especially as Harrison wants to win it for his Papa, whom he 'can't wait to tell' (231).

Chapter Thirty Nine

We hear that Auntie Sonia has left Julius. Harrison's mother invites Sonia to stay into she finds 'somewhere else' (232). Both women seem to be in a dangerous predicament, as Harrison's mother feels involved in Julius's business 'ever since' she 'took his money' (232).

The narrator gives us hope from the natural world, by informing us that 'if a skink gets his tail bitten off he just grows a new one' (233). It's just nature's way of saying never give up.

As well as being shocked at the word 'Dead' etched on his front door, Harrison is also surprised to learn that Auntie Sonia's small tree is 'only plastic' (234). Harrison adapts to the revelation by saying that 'a plastic tree is only a lie if it pretends to be a real tree (234).

The subject switches to superheroes with Harrison admiring Altaf's drawing of 'Lion Man' (235). This suggests Harrison is full of pride and courage.

Harrison explains to Altaf that 'Snake Man' is 'real' (236). He is still haunted by images of the video which he saw earlier in the narrative.

Chapter Forty

Discussion of the English language dominates the beginning of this chapter, as Harrison explains that 'when something sucks it means it's the worst' (237). He acknowledges that the term comes 'from America', which recognises the living nature of the language (237).

Later, along with Dean, he tries to use Lydia's phone to 'catch' the dead boy's 'spirit on camera' (238). While doing this, Harrison recollects how X-Fire 'kept calling' the dead boy 'a poser', after 'he scored a basket from one end of the court to the other' (239). The dead boy fought his corner, going as far as spitting 'all' of his big drink 'on Killa's back' (240). Perhaps that provided the motive for the killing.

Harrison and Dean get cornered by the gang in the basketball court, and unfortunately the former drops a picture of the dead boy. Killa stares at it as if he was 'trying to make it disappear'. He seems as if he is overcome with guilt or fear of being found out.

X-Fire blames Killa for the murder, saying: 'You got us into this' (242). He kicks Killa's behind and the latter runs exactly like the actual killer when he starts running away with 'his elbows [...] sticking out like a girl' (242).

Meanwhile, Lydia's phone which was dropped during the altercation falls into the hands of the owner, who films the whole episode (including the burning of the dead boy's photograph). Lydia, Harrison and Dean run into the sanctuary offered by 'the big library' to email the video to Abena 'for extra security' (243). It seems that education (represented by the library) is something worth worshipping in the harsh world that they live in; at least that offers real salvation in the here and now.

The last words in the chapter are reserved for the pigeon who describes humans as 'just meat loosely wrapped around a blazing star' (244). This seems to mean that once a human dies that dead person can experience real freedom as a star in the heavens.

Chapter Forty One

The chapter begins with Connor Green breaking the spell and ruining everyone's summer holidays by stepping 'on a crack' (245). To make matters worse, he reveals that he witnessed the murder; he says: 'I seen the kid get stabbed and I seen Jermaine Bent running away' (245).

Harrison finds this news incredulous as he reveals: 'I couldn't believe it' (246). He adds that he keeps 'hoping there was another Jermaine Bent who wasn't Killa' (246). Although all the evidence points to Killa, Harrison is refusing to accept the obvious. He'd rather live in the security of his imaginary world.

He retreats to that place while running around the school playing field. He decides that if he eats 'crab apples' he can 'get all the superpowers' that he needs (247). Although he recognises they are 'poison for the others' he convinces himself that for him 'it's a meteor' (247).

His determination to become 'Unstoppable Man' is tarnished somewhat by his 'belly' feeling 'proper bad after' eating the crab apples (248).

Chapter Forty Two

The chapter begins ominously with the words: 'The war was here' (249). It seems like a war zone as everyone watches 'the playground die' (249). The burning of the playground seems to indicate that the time for playing is over; from now on, it's going to grown-up and more serious. This feeling is emphasised by the personification of the playground.

Nevertheless, Harrison tries to take something positive out of the destruction. He says: 'It made you feel like you were together' (250). The use of direct address makes the reader feel part of the scene too, emphasising the togetherness felt by all present.

Even the water that quells the fire seems violent, as Harrison describes it as 'superquick like a bullet' (251). The aftermath of the fire is just as dangerous-sounding, as we are told of 'a piece of dead rope', which looks 'just like a snake' (252).

The pigeon ends the narrative in this chapter, walking 'around the ruins of the playground' (253). It says it was hoping for 'a last-minute change of plan' (253). We can only hope that the pigeon will be instrumental in the downfall of the murderers.

Chapter Forty Three

The warlike environment shows few signs of changing, as the school students pretend they are 'ninjas' on the last day of the summer term (254).

Harrison is enjoying the moment, especially the Year 11 'tradition' of writing good luck messages on each others' shirts (255). He is a traditionalist at heart and is looking forward to being that age so he can experience the same.

We then are treated to some of the messages on the shirts, which include 'GET RICH OR DIE TRYIN' (256). This is a reference to 50 Cent's film debut, which is about a gangster trying to make it in a harsh urban world. It is also about materialism or the importance of making money.

There is a more hopeful message in lower case letters, that reads: 'we are all made of stars' (257). This indicates a belief that there is a place reserved in heaven for our souls once we pass away.

Chapter Forty Four

The Year 11s get out of school first and start 'a big water fight' (258). The other students 'can't wait to be let out' too (258). They all shout: 'They want freedom' (258).

However, when they get out they escape the security offered by school. The outside is fraught with danger but excitement. This excitement with a hint of danger is exemplified when Harrison reveals that Poppy's beauty makes his 'belly' turns 'over like an aeroplane' (259).

The name Poppy, of course, makes the reader think of all the dead people in the two world wars. Her kiss could be the kiss of death, but Harrison says her 'breath' is 'the only superpower' he needs (260).

There seems to be no real escape from the hell he lives in, though. This is shown by 'the dead climbing frame' (261). Rather than allowing people to climb out of poverty, this environment only offers death as a release and freedom. Even 'a tree' is depicted 'in a cage' (261)

Ironically, the stairs that Harrison believes are 'safe' are where his attacker waits for him (261). After the stabbing, all he can 'taste' is metal (262).

The special pigeon tells Harrison that he'll 'be going home soon' (263). It seems that the pigeon's job is to simply to reassure and guide the dead in the right direction: presumably to heaven.

Essay writing tips

<u>Use a variety of connectives</u>

Have a look of this list of connectives. Which of these would you choose to use?

'ADDING' DISCOURSE MARKERS

- AND

- ALSO

- AS WELL AS

- MOREOVER

- TOO

- FURTHERMORE

- ADDITIONALLY

I hope you chose 'additionally', 'furthermore' and 'moreover'. Don't be afraid to use the lesser discourse markers, as they are also useful. Just avoid using those ones over and over again. I've seen essays from Key Stage 4 students that use the same discourse marker for the opening sentence of each paragraph! Needless to say, those essays didn't get great marks!

Okay, here are some more connectives for you to look at. Select the best ones.

'SEQUENCING' DISCOURSE MARKERS

- NEXT

- FIRSTLY

- SECONDLY

- THIRDLY

- FINALLY

- MEANWHILE

- AFTER

- THEN

- SUBSEQUENTLY

This time, I hope you chose 'subsequently' and 'meanwhile'.

Here are some more connectives for you to 'grade'!

'ILLUSTRATING / EXEMPLIFYING' DISCOURSE MARKERS

- FOR EXAMPLE

- SUCH AS

- FOR INSTANCE

- IN THE CASE OF

- AS REVEALED BY

- ILLUSTRATED BY

I'd probably go for 'illustrated by' or even 'as exemplified by' (which is not in the list!). Please feel free to add your own examples to the lists. Strong connectives impress examiners. Don't forget it! That's why I want you to look at some more.

'CAUSE & EFFECT' DISCOURSE MARKERS

- BECAUSE
- SO
- THEREFORE
- THUS
- CONSEQUENTLY
- HENCE

I'm going for 'consequently' this time. How about you? What about the next batch?

'COMPARING' DISCOURSE MARKERS

- SIMILARLY
- LIKEWISE
- AS WITH
- LIKE
- EQUALLY
- IN THE SAME WAY

I'd choose 'similarly' this time. Still some more to go.

'QUALIFYING' DISCOURSE MARKERS

- BUT

- HOWEVER
- WHILE
- ALTHOUGH
- UNLESS
- EXCEPT
- APART FROM
- AS LONG AS

It's 'however' for me!

'CONTRASTING' DISCOURSE MARKERS

- WHEREAS
- INSTEAD OF
- ALTERNATIVELY
- OTHERWISE
- UNLIKE
- ON THE OTHER HAND
- CONVERSELY

I'll take 'conversely' or 'alternatively' this time.

'EMPHASISING' DISCOURSE MARKERS

- ABOVE ALL
- IN PARTICULAR

- ESPECIALLY

- SIGNIFICANTLY

- INDEED

- NOTABLY

You can breathe a sigh of relief now! It's over! No more connectives. However, now I want to put our new found skills to use in our essays.

Useful information/Glossary

Allegory: extended metaphor, like the grim reaper representing death, e.g. Scrooge symbolizing capitalism.

Alliteration: same consonant sound repeating, e.g. 'She sells sea shells'.

Allusion: reference to another text/person/place/event.

Ascending tricolon: sentence with three parts, each increasing in power, e.g. 'ringing, drumming, shouting'.

Aside: character speaking so some characters cannot hear what is being said. Sometimes, an aside is directly to the audience. It's a dramatic technique which reveals the character's inner thoughts and feelings.

Assonance: same vowel sounds repeating, e.g. 'Oh no, won't Joe go?'

Bathos: abrupt change from sublime to ridiculous for humorous effect.

Blank verse: lines of unrhymed iambic pentameter.

Compressed time: when the narrative is fast-forwarding through the action.

Descending tricolon: sentence with three parts, each decreasing in power, e.g. 'shouting, talking, whispering'.

Denouement: tying up loose ends, the resolution.

Diction: choice of words or vocabulary.

Didactic: used to describe literature designed to inform, instruct or pass on a moral message.

Dilated time: opposite compressed time, here the narrative is in slow motion.

Direct address: second person narrative, predominantly using the personal pronoun 'you'.

Dramatic action verb: manifests itself in physical action, e.g. I punched him in the face.

Dramatic irony: audience knows something that the character is unaware of.

Ellipsis: leaving out part of the story and allowing the reader to fill in the narrative gap.

End-stopped lines: poetic lines that end with punctuation.

Epistolary: letter or correspondence-driven narrative.

Flashback/Analepsis: going back in time to the past, interrupting the chronological sequence.

Flashforward/Prolepsis: going forward in time to the future, interrupting the chronological sequence.

Foreshadowing/Adumbrating: suggestion of plot developments that will occur later in the narrative.

Gothic: another strand of Romanticism, typically with a wild setting, a sensitive heroine, an older man with a 'piercing gaze', discontinuous structure, doppelgangers, guilt and the 'unspeakable' (according to Eve Kosofsky Sedgwick).

Hamartia: character flaw, leading to that character's downfall.

Hyperbole: exaggeration for effect.

Iambic pentameter: a line of ten syllables beginning with a lighter stress alternating with a heavier stress in its perfect form, which sounds like a heartbeat. The stress falls on the even syllables, numbers: 2, 4, 6, 8 and 10, e.g. 'When now I think you can behold such sights'.

Intertextuality: links to other literary texts.

Irony: amusing or cruel reversal of expected outcome or words meaning the opposite to their literal meaning.

Metafiction/Romantic irony: self-conscious exposure of the devices used to create 'the truth' within a work of fiction.

Motif: recurring image use of language or idea that connects the narrative together and creates a theme or mood, e.g. 'green light' in *The Great Gatsby*.

Oxymoron: contradictory terms combined, e.g. deafening silence.

Pastiche: imitation of another's work.

Pathetic fallacy: a form of personification whereby inanimate objects show human attributes, e.g. 'the sea smiled benignly'. The originator of the term, John Ruskin in 1856, used 'the cruel, crawling foam', from Kingsley's *The Sands of Dee*, as an example to clarify what he meant by the 'morbid' nature of pathetic fallacy.

Personification: concrete or abstract object made human, often simply achieved by using a capital letter or a personal pronoun, e.g. 'Nature', or describing a ship as 'she'.

Pun/Double entendre: a word with a double meaning, usually employed in witty wordplay but not always.

Retrospective: account of events after they have occurred.

Romanticism: genre celebrating the power of imagination, spriritualism and nature.

Semantic/lexical field: related words about a single concept, e.g. king, queen and prince are all concerned with royalty.

Soliloquy: character thinks aloud, but is not heard by other characters (unlike in a monologue) giving the audience access to inner thoughts and feelings.

Style: choice of language, form and structure, and effects produced.

Synecdoche: one part of something referring to the whole, e.g. Carker's teeth represent him in *Dombey and Son*.

Syntax: the way words and sentences are placed together.

Tetracolon climax: sentence with four parts, culminating with the last part, e.g. 'I have nothing to offer but blood, toil, tears, and sweat ' (Winston Churchill).

ABOUT THE AUTHOR

Joe Broadfoot is a secondary school teacher of English and a soccer journalist, who also writes fiction and literary criticism. His former experiences as a DJ took him to far-flung places such as Tokyo, Kobe, Beijing, Hong Kong, Jakarta, Cairo, Dubai, Cannes, Oslo, Bergen and Bodo. He is now PGCE and CELTA-qualified with QTS, a first-class honours degree in Literature and an MA in Victorian Studies (majoring in Charles Dickens). Drama is close to his heart as he acted in 'Macbeth' and 'A Midsummer Night's Dream' at the Royal Northern College of Music in Manchester. More recently, he has been teaching 'A' Level and GCSE English Literature and IGCSE and GCSE English Language to students at secondary schools in Buckinghamshire, Kent and in south and west London.

Printed in Great Britain
by Amazon